"I'M RIGHT AND YOU'RE WRONG!"

WHY WE DISAGREE ABOUT THE BIBLE AND WHAT TO DO ABOUT IT

BY

STEVE KINDLE

Energion Publications
Gonzalez, FL
2015

ISBN10: 1-63199-099-3
ISBN13: 978-1-63199-099-1

Energion Publications
P. O. Box 841
Gonzalez, FL 32560

energion.com
pubs@energion.com

Dedicated to the memory of
John Sterling
who held deep convictions
while embracing all people

With thanks and appreciation to Larry Haight, Director of Library Services, and Eric Wheeler, Reader and Digital Services Librarian for Simpson University, and Keegan Osinski, Public Services Assistant, Vanderbilt Divinity Library, for their assistance in providing many of the resources for this book.

INTRODUCTION

How many times have you had a conversation with someone that involved a disagreement over the Bible? And how many times have these conversations led to interruptions of friendships or even extended family disputes? Some of these disputes have split congregations. Even the more mild disagreements can leave us perplexed. Why is it that something so plain to one is so obviously unconvincing to others? This often leads us to search for ways to convince others through honing our interpretive skills, doing elaborate word studies, consulting scholarly commentaries and the like. In the end, however, people don't easily change their minds, and we are left to wonder why.

This book differs from most in that rather than looking at how to interpret the Bible properly, we'll examine the sources of disagreement among interpreters. We all have our own ways of trying to understand the Bible and they are close to our hearts. Many of us think our way is superior to most, if not all. But we will not venture into who is right and who is wrong in our interpretations. What concerns us here is why we interpret the way we do and what our attitude should be toward those with whom we disagree.

The current landscape of biblical disagreement is literally worldwide. After nearly two millennia of serious-minded interpreters diligently studying the Bible, we are in alarming disarray. This would not be so serious except for the reality that differences of interpretation can run so deep that, in the extreme, Christians have killed other Christians[1], and less so, many denominational bodies have separated, even condemned to hell, those with whom they disagree. Nothing demonstrates this more than the 33,000 Christian denominations identified in the World Christian Encyclopedia (2001, 2nd edition). While not all of these separated themselves out of theological or interpretive differences, thousands did.

---

1   On Boston Common, a statue stands in memory of Mary Dyer, a Quaker who refused to disavow her beliefs, and was hanged by Puritans in 1660, because it was illegal to be a Quaker in Massachusetts.

Here's a brief listing of some of the areas with no consensus that continue to divide Christendom: original sin, mode of baptism, purpose of baptism, the Trinity, present role of the Holy Spirit, how to be saved, is there a hell, all the millennial reign issues, women's role in the church and society, universal or limited salvation, war and pacifism, faith and works, justification, sanctification, gay issues, appropriate church polity, how to understand the Lord's Supper (Communion, Eucharist), when to observe the Lord's Supper, who should receive the Lord's Supper, Apostolic succession, Theory of Evolution, interpreting the book of Revelation, the historicity of Adam and Eve, is the future open or preordained, the death penalty, abortion, euthanasia … on and on we could go. Some of these positions have divided churches, families, even nations. These are of continuing concern as we seek to live together in our churches, homes and communities.

The ways in which these issues are dealt with is the subject of this book. Every one of the positions taken to bring clarity to these issues is not made in a vacuum; they all arise out of the prevailing conditions of the day and are products of influences we are not always aware of. That is as true for me as it is for you. So let's take a look at the highlights of the history of interpretation, or what could be called a history of disagreement.

CHAPTER 1
A (SHORT) HISTORY OF DISAGREEMENT

A (BRIEF) HISTORY OF BIBLICAL INTERPRETATION

The history of biblical interpretation is, among other things, a history of disagreements. The contents of this section will of necessity be arbitrary and overly limited. I chose to feature representative samples of the more important interpretive moves and hope that they will serve to illustrate the larger history.

It's no surprise that biblical arguments arose from the very beginning of conversations about the Bible, but it comes as a surprise to many that the Bible even argues with itself. I will just give two of the more generally received examples, one from each Testament. The theology of the book of Deuteronomy lays out a clear call to obedience to the Law of God. For those who follow the Law, it promises God will provide health, prosperity, abundant descendants, and, in the case of Israel, protection from its enemies. Both Job and Ecclesiastes were written to challenge that theology. The Preacher in Ecclesiastes surveys his life and observes that just the opposite seems to prevail. The righteous poor are oppressed and the rich are the oppressors. He finally concludes that it's better to obey than not, even though it remains a mystery why.

In the New Testament, the apostle Paul stakes out a very clear position that salvation is by faith alone, as in Ephesians 2:8-9, "For by grace you have been saved through faith, and this is not your own doing; it is the gift of God—not the result of works, so that no one may boast." On the other hand, James concludes his section on the place of works by declaring, "You see that a person is justified by works and not by faith alone." Some say these positions can be made complementary, yet others do not. The champion of *sola fide* (faith alone), Martin Luther, called James "an epistle of straw." He apparently read James against Paul. These are just two examples of how the Bible was interpreted from within. If following the Bible is your rule, you now have permission to question it, perhaps even disagree with it, but most of all you must interpret it.

Moving into the post-Apostolic era, roughly the first half of the second century, it is clear that scripture was the place the church looked to for answers. But this was before the Canon (the sixty-six books of the Christian Bible) was universally known and agreed upon. This period is notable for its plethora of competing beliefs, as what eventually became known as orthodoxy[2] (correct belief) was yet to prevail. Largely, conclusions were drawn from the Old Testament, specifically, the Greek version known as the Septuagint (LXX). As more of the writings that would comprise the New Testament became known and recognized, they too were added to the repository of consulted texts. However, the conclusions found when consulting scripture were often incomprehensible to the interpreters involved.[3] The church argued over the precise nature of Jesus; was he truly human or only seemed to be? Is the end of the world near or not? How can true meaning be derived; is it literal or spiritual, or both? When should we celebrate Easter? Has the age of miracles ceased? Who are fit subjects for baptism? Are bishops rightly the direct successors to the apostles? Is the church the "new Israel," superseding it, or in continuity with it?

By far, though, the most pressing question was how to connect the story of the Old Testament to the church. The methods of interpretation varied, as well. By this time, the Greco-Roman myths of the gods had largely lost their literal meaning and were being reinterpreted allegorically.[4] This was true not only of Olympus, but of Homer as well. Early Christian thinkers inherited this way of approaching ancient stories and began to use the Old Testament

---

2   Orthodoxy or Orthodox, when capitalized, usually refers to the Eastern Orthodox Church.

3   Tertullian's famous dictum, "What has Athens to do with Jerusalem, or the Academy with the Church?" (*De praescriptione*, vii). Athens represented non-Christian philosophers, yet many of the early apologists worked from their systems.

4   Allegory is an extended metaphor that finds associations deeper than the literal meaning.

in the same way. (Paul had earlier used allegory to gain meaning from the story of Sarah and Hagar in Galatians to point to the old and new covenants God made with God's people.) The Jewish philosopher, Philo, Paul's contemporary, treated much of the Old Testament in this way.

But allegorical interpretations were capable of wide ranging associations that often strayed so far from the meaning of the text that many were concerned it was proving anything and therefore nothing. What ultimately saved interpreters from fantastical or heretical outcomes was the Rule of Faith popularized by Irenaeus of Lyons (130—202 CE) and considered the beginning of emerging orthodoxy.[5] If you are familiar with the Apostle's and Nicene Creeds, you will note The Rule's influence on them. Here's the significant paragraph:

> "To this order many nations of barbarians give assent . . . believing in one God, Maker of heaven and earth, and all that in them is, through Christ Jesus the Son of God; Who, for his astounding love towards his creatures, sustained the birth of the Virgin, himself uniting his manhood to God, and suffered under Pontius Pilate, and rose again, and was received in glory, shall come in glory, the Savior of those who are saved, and the judge of those who are judged; and sending into eternal fire the perverters of the truth and the despisers of his Father and his advent."[6]

As long as allegorical interpreters stayed within The Rule, their outcomes were under proper control (at least as orthodox interpreters were concerned) and predictable, if not always enlightening.

Augustine (354-430 CE) often used allegory to interpret stories about Jesus. One memorable interpretation involves the story of Jesus walking on the water. Why, he asks, were the disciples not able to walk as Jesus had? They needed a boat to carry them across the water. The wood of the boat is, in truth, the wood of the cross, which carries disciples safely to heaven. (I bet you missed that!)

---

5   Henry Wansbrough, OSB, *The Use and Abuse of the Bible*, (London: T&T Clark, 2010), p.26.
6   *Against Heresies*, Book III, Chapter 4, 1-2.

Noah's ark was the subject of much allegorical speculation. Hugh of St. Victor (12th Century) found that the length of the arc at three hundred cubits represented the cross as, in Greek rendering, T stood for three hundred, and T was shaped in the form of the cross. Therefore, the arc which took Noah and his family to safety points to the cross of Christ which carries Christians to their salvation. In this way, the Old and New Testaments were seen to be teaching the same things.

The Church of the Roman Empire was organically and politically one church up to the Great Schism of 1054 when the Western pope and the Eastern patriarch excommunicated each other and their churches. Thus the Roman Catholic and Eastern Orthodox churches were born. Yes, they had very major disagreements along the way, but behind them all was a deep difference in their worldviews. According to Gerald Bray, "Many of the later differences between West and East can be explained by the fact that the former adopted the linear view of history and the latter the cyclical, and each read the Bible accordingly."[7]If the lenses you wear tell you the sky is blue and your neighbor's say the sky is green, you will eventually quit talking altogether.

A significant controversy that confronted the church before doctrinal consensus was achieved and then broken asunder by the Protestant Reformation (1517-1648 CE) was over millenarianism, the belief that Jesus would return to Earth and rule over his kingdom for 1000 years. Following which, the general resurrection would take place and Jesus would judge the living and the dead. Some of the most influential proponents were Justin Martyr, Polycarp, Mileto of Sardis, and Montanus. Other very influential leaders of this period, including Tertullian, were likely candidates for sainthood except for this belief. They based their beliefs on a combination of the book of Revelation and some non-canonical writings of the period, such as the Shepherd of Hermas. Some linked the petition in the Lord's Prayer for the kingdom to come with the penultimate statement in the book of Revelation, "Come,

---

7   Gerald Bray, *Biblical Interpretation*, (Downers Grove, Illinois: InterVarsity Press, 1996), p.99.

Lord Jesus," indicating that the millennial reign of Revelation chapter 20 was about to take place. If this sounds familiar, these interpretive skirmishes continue to our day.

The interpreters of the Middle Ages devised what they called "the four senses of scripture," the literal, allegorical, anagogical, and moral meanings.[8] The literal conveys the sense the author wished to convey, the allegorical sense was a way to derive doctrinal meaning by turning the literal text (a boat, e.g.) into a spiritual metaphor (the cross), as we've seen above. The anagogical (literally "leading upward") sense spiritualizes the text so that it points to the next life. In this way, crossing the river Jordan becomes death, the transition from this world to the next. The moral sense helps to discover the proper way of life hidden in the literal sense. Augustine summarized the significance of the four senses: "The Letter speaks of deeds; Allegory to faith; The Moral how to act; Anagogy our destiny."[9]

The two leading biblical interpreters up through the Middle Ages were Augustine (354-430 CE) and Thomas Aquinas (1225-1274 CE). This is as good a place as any to underscore the notion that interpretations of the Bible are not made in a vacuum. It fact, it is not saying too much that no interpretation is free of outside influences, a topic we will pursue in Chapter 2. In the case of these two giants, Augustine was influenced by Platonic philosophy and Aquinas by Aristotelian philosophy. For Augustine, to cite one example, following Plato, knowledge comes by way of recollection. The souls of humans were once with God before being born on Earth, and proper understanding, or faith in God, will be given to those who seek it through the Christian teachings. They will "recollect" what they once knew of God. However, truth will necessarily not be absolute, as creatures cannot fully comprehend the Creator. Aquinas, following Aristotle, was much more given to seeking truth through the senses, since according to Aristotle, there is nothing to recollect and the "real" is not in heaven but inheres in the objects themselves. Therefore, Augustine was much more inclined toward

---

8   Henri du Lubac. *Medieval Exegesis: The Four Senses of Scripture*, Vol. 1, (Grand Rapids: Eerdmans, 1998), p.15ff.
9   St. Augustine, *Contra Epistolam Manichaei* 5, 6: PL 42, 176.

allegory and Aquinas toward a more literal understanding of the text as acquired by one's reason.

This led to quite different outcomes that each took to biblical interpretation. For example, the meaning of "This is my body" in the liturgy of the Lord's Supper hinges on Plato vs. Aristotle. For Augustine, since the "real" existed in heaven with God, it could only be represented here on earth, so bread was bread and wine was wine. Jesus' real body was in heaven. With Aquinas, the bread and wine could become the body and blood of Jesus (Transubstantiation) because there was no representative/symbolic meaning to be derived from bread. Therefore, it can become fully the body and blood of Jesus. They were looking at the same words, but because they were working from different perspectives, they found different meaning. So you see that we take with us many influences that shape how we understand the Bible.

As we move into the Protestant Reformation, we are confronted with the most serious overturning of biblical beliefs since the Roman Catholic Church defined the content of the faith. Up to then, the Church relied not so much on scripture but on the presumed interpretation of scripture taught by those officially in the line of Apostolic Succession (Bishops) and approved Church Tradition, that is, extra-biblical teachings held sacred. The Reformers jettisoned Tradition and famously declared that one should be guided by the Bible alone (sola scriptura). Since no one is guided simply by the Bible alone, but by interpretations derived from the Bible which may or may not comply with proper meaning, a plethora of interpretations sprang up all over Europe.[10] The end result is the multiplicity of denominations and sects scattered throughout the world as seen in our day.

The Bible for centuries was thought to be above human scrutiny. It was even thought that the Greek of the New Testament was a special "Holy Spirit" Greek that existed nowhere else on Earth,

---

10   I can't find the source, but I remember reading that a pope of this era remarked, "With every man his own Bible, soon every man his own church." Whoever he was, he was prophetic!

given by God for its unique use in the Bible.[11] With the discoveries of well-preserved papyri in the 18th and 19th centuries, scholars soon found that Greek similar to biblical Greek was the language of "the common people," as opposed to the literary authors of the day, who used a higher form of Greek. Since the common people didn't write much, there was little to go on until masses of papyri revealed grocery lists, love letters, and the like, that conformed to the Greek of the New Testament. Consequently, it's called Koine (Common) Greek.

Along with the Enlightenment's new-found enthusiasm for scientific research based on evidence, this made it possible to look at the Bible the same way scholars looked at other documents of antiquity...by looking for its sources, authors, historicity, dates, and other critical pursuits. (Keep in mind that "critical" is not a pejorative, but a technique of inquiry that is based on rigorous investigation and peer review. A theater critic, after all, may critically judge a play an overwhelming success as well as a flop.) This created approaches to biblical interpretation heretofore not seen, such as the Documentary Hypothesis, Source, Literary, Form, Redaction, Rhetorical, Canonical, Narrative, Psychological, Textual, Socio-scientific, Postmodernist, Liberation, and Feminist criticisms, to name but a few. Not to worry—the critical scholarly feuds are not our concern here.[12] Although they help us understand the Bible, they go beyond the scope of this book. We will concentrate on why you and I may not see the Bible the same way, why that may be, and what we can do about it.

Biblical interpretation in the modern era will follow (below) with our discussion of Evangelicalism, Liberalism, Fundamentalism, Pentecostalism, and Progressive theology.

The result of nearly 2000 years of pondering over the Bible is to find us today standing not far from the early period of church

11   Hermann Cremer, *Biblico-Theological Lexicon of New Testament Greek*, (London: T&T Clark, 1895) p. iv.
12   If it is your concern, a good place to start is with Steven L. McKenzie & Stephen R. Haynes, *To Each His Own Meaning*, (Louisville: Westminster John Knox Press, 1999). It provides overviews of modern critical methods.

history where there was no consensus of core biblical teaching. You'd think we would have learned by now that if the quest for clarity and unity of thought is not exactly impossible, it is daunting and should sober us up to the reality that something is very wrong, especially with our attitudes about our own beliefs.

This survey, short as it is, should make us aware of at least two realities. One, that the Bible has never *not* been interpreted and reinterpreted; and two, that differences among interpreters, even profound differences, have existed from the very beginning. Some were considered benign, merely matters of opinion; others created schisms that exist into to our own day. Different ways of interpreting the Bible that yield differing outcomes have always existed and will always exist. It's certain that the "assured results" of today's interpreters will be revised and even overturned by tomorrow's. The question for us, it seems to me, is not who is right, but the kind of attitude we should take about our own and other's results.

The third reality is this: the Bible needs to be interpreted; it does not speak clearly and unequivocally for itself, at least much of the time. If it were easily understood and clearly so, we would not have such differing and contradictory understandings among well-intentioned and erudite people. The notion that "the Bible said it, I believe it, and that settles it," is to confuse what one reader thinks it means with what it actually means. No. Interpretation is not only necessary, it is inevitable. That's why it's so important that we understand how and why disagreements arise and our own susceptibility to faulty interpretations. We now turn to that discussion.

CHAPTER 2
WHY WE DISAGREE

Being born into your world is like moving into a fully furnished house that was completely designed, decorated, and landscaped with no input from you. No thought was given to your taste, interests, preferences, needs or desires. You had no say whatsoever in any regard to your new abode. Our individual part of the world is like that. We had no choice as to our country of origin, language, form of government, even our religion. All of these preceded us in our world. The child's whine that "It's not fair!" is our first recognition of this reality. No, the world is not set up with us in mind.

The world we inhabit presents itself to us as the "givens," the things we take for granted, the things that "just are the way they are." I doubt you worry too much that the sun may not rise tomorrow, or that the laws of aerodynamics may change mid-flight. Most of us reading this are well-situated in our Newtonian universe.

Generally speaking, we seldom give much thought to how we live, or why we do the things we do, or why things are the way they are. We accept our "houses" as they are presented to us and generally don't object to much that is there. We easily accommodate the world around us, and this has been true from the beginning of human life.

But the "houses" that people are born into have changed over the millennia. Today we know the Earth circles the sun, but most of our ancestors thought the Earth was the center of the universe. It's only recently that the germ theory of disease replaced miasma, or "bad air" as the cause of most illnesses. In Jesus' time, sin was often seen as the cause of blindness and most infirmities. The notion that thunder and lightning, rain, drought, earthquakes, and eclipses are the products of the gods have vanished except in the most primitive societies.

For most of human history, people lived with widely shared beliefs about their world in close-knit communities. Those who saw the world differently were outsiders, strangers to be avoided and to be suspicious of. They usually lived in other countries, worshiped other gods, and their boundaries were well-defined. Seldom were they crossed except by necessity.

Today, our world is organized quite differently. Although its dimensions have been constant, we find that, culturally and technologically, it's a "small world," even a global village. It is characterized by people of radically different notions of how the world works living side by side. No longer is it necessary to travel distances to engage people who differ from your own; they live next door. This is known as pluralism, which the Miriam-Webster Dictionary defines as "a situation in which people of different social classes, religions, races, etc., are together in a society but continue to have their different traditions and interests." Additionally, pluralism encourages understanding and celebrating differences rather than anathematizing them as in the past.[13]

This house that we are born into and shapes the way we think and live is often referred to as a worldview. Here are a couple of definitions. From James W. Sire, a worldview is "a set of presuppositions (assumptions which may be true, partially true or entirely false) which we hold (consciously or subconsciously, consistently or inconsistently) about the basic makeup of our world."[14] He adds, these presuppositions "work together to provide a more or less coherent frame of reference for all thought and action."[15] James Olthuis puts it this way, "A worldview (or vision of life) is a framework or set of fundamental beliefs through which we view the world and our calling and future in it.... It is the integrative and interpretive framework by which order and disorder are judged; it is the standard by which reality is managed and pursued; it is the set of hinges on which all our everyday thinking and doing turns."[16] In short, our worldviews are the lenses through which we

---

13   The reality of pluralism is captured beautifully in the title of a book on worldviews, *The Universe Next Door*, by James W. Sire, (Downers Grove, Illinois: InterVarsity Press), 3rd ed., 1976.
14   Sire, *ibid.*, p. 16.
15   Sire, *ibid.*, p. 15.
16   James Olthuis, *Stained Glass: Worldviews and Social Science*, ed. Paul A. Marshall et al, "Christian Studies Today," p. 29.

view the world. None of us is born with perfect vision; we all suffer from worldview myopia, and unlike physical eyesight, there is no corrective lens that can make us comprehend the world perfectly.

It needs to be stated very forcefully and unequivocally that NO ONE looks at the world lens free. Although our "world houses" are all arranged differently, we all inhabit one. That means that all of us share one thing in common: our worlds, of necessity, will be seen differently. We cannot escape this; it is part of the human condition. This is one of the major reasons we see the Bible differently, and why those differences are often incomprehensible from another point of view.

EXAMPLES OF HOW WORLDVIEWS SHAPE OUR "REALITY"

Lest we get off to a bad start, since I chose to place quotation marks around "reality," I want to assure you that I believe in truth, Truth and Ultimate Truth. Do I believe I fully comprehend truth? Or you? No, not in the ultimate sense. Being finite beings, we are incapable of comprehending ultimate truth. We can touch the hem of its garment, be guided in wholesome ways, and find meaningful interpretations that transcend our presumed reality and force us to redirect our lives. But I don't possess absolute truth and I don't think you do either. For many, the "Great Confession" of Peter in Matthew 16:16, "You are the Messiah, the Son of the living God," serves as the highest expression of Truth found in the Bible. In fact, Jesus congratulates Peter on this insight as coming straight from God. So we would be entitled to believe that the confessor of the great confession knew what he was talking about. But we find the very opposite is true. In explaining what it means that Jesus is the Messiah, Jesus announces that he must go to Jerusalem and be put to death. Peter objects so strenuously that Jesus now accuses Peter of acting in the place of Satan. So it's one thing to say (or read) the words and quite another to fully comprehend what they mean.

Perhaps another incident will help clear up what I mean. Since every word you read or hear is processed through a filtering system or lens, everyone reads or hears the same word or words differently. Depending on how far apart our systems are, we can basically understand each other or totally misunderstand. In explaining this to an adult Sunday School class, one member said, "I can think of something in the Bible we both read that needs no filtering, that is straightforward and immediately understood." "Okay," I said. "Let's have it." He responded, "God is love." I replied with, "What do you mean by 'God' and what do you mean by 'love'"? He got my point. We have already seen how the worldviews of two Greek philosophers, Plato and Aristotle, influenced Augustine and Aquinas, and how different their approaches to biblical interpretation were because of this. Worldviews matter, even if you don't realize you have one.

Before Copernicus' heliocentric theory (the Earth and other planets revolve around the sun) was accepted, people took for granted that the sun moved around the Earth. This is reflected in biblical passages such as Psalm 93:4b-6, *In the heavens he has set a tent for the sun, which comes out like a bridegroom from his wedding canopy, and like a strong man runs its course with joy. Its rising is from the end of the heavens, and its circuit to the end of them; and nothing is hid from its heat.* Interpreters with this view of the world had no problem taking it literally. After Copernicus and Galileo, this is no longer possible. Virtually all biblical interpreters accept the heliocentric view.

Unanimity is not the case, however, regarding how to date the age of the Earth. Before the Theory of Evolution, it was quite reasonable to accept Bishop Ussher's date of the beginning of creation as October 23, 4004 BC. Geologists now estimate the age of the Earth at approximately 4.5 billion years. Interpreters who view Genesis 1 as a science text and take it literally, will hold to a "young Earth." Those who see Genesis 1 as a poetic ode to God's creative spirit will not. Why the difference? Your worldview accommodates the Theory or it doesn't.

INTERPRETIVE MODELS

Interpretive models are derived from our worldviews and function in much the same way: they order our thoughts and control the outcomes. The following is a representative list of the major

14

interpretive categories within Christendom. It is certainly not exhaustive, but will serve to illustrate how we make hermeneutical and exegetical decisions based on previously accepted norms. Hermeneutics generally means the broad principles of interpretation; exegesis is the application of those principles. Hermeneutics takes its name from the Greek god Hermes who was the messenger of the gods to humans. Exegesis is from the Greek word meaning "to lead out" the meaning of the text and is the opposite of eisegesis, "to draw into" or import meanings from outside the text. In a way, all exegesis is driven from a point of view and is in one way or another eisegesis. It is also unavoidable.

Interpretive models include what are called *a priori* assumptions. These are the often unexamined "givens" that we take for granted which may or may not be true. We interpret Psalm 93 from a heliocentric point of view because prior to coming to the text we understand the operation of the sun in that way. Likewise, a white bigot prejudges all black people as inferior prior to ever meeting one. The validity of outcomes depends largely on the validity of our interpretive models and their assumptions.

Here's a way of looking at this. Consider these sums: $1+1=3+2=5+6=11+5=16+4=20$. Every sum is the correct answer except for $1+1=3$. So even though everything is correct after the first move, the answer is wrong because it began on a false move. So when we examine interpretations, unless we know on what basis the interpretation is made, we may be dazzled by the brilliance of the exegesis but misled by its conclusion. We also need to know our own biases as well. The best an interpreter can do is to acknowledge one's own biases and clearly identify how they impact an interpretation.

Interpretations are always and inevitably a product of one's worldview, assumptions, temperament, and time and place. Working together they provide the rich soil out of which interpretations spring. With this in mind, we now turn to examining the dominant approaches to biblical interpretation that inform most of Christianity today.

Regardless of the theological positions held, they mostly spring from one or more of the areas expressed in the Wesleyan Quadrilateral:[17] scripture, tradition, experience and reason. How one finally interprets the Bible is determined by which of the four is most emphasized. For most Christians, the authority of the Bible is foundational, yet there is no consensus as to how that authority is derived. Tradition, experience and reason are means of determining that authority.

Tradition seeks to listen to the acquired wisdom of the church through the ages. It can't be authoritative in itself, because there are many voices expressing diverse opinions. Yet, knowledge of how our predecessors viewed things keeps us from forming our opinions in a vacuum. Peter wrote *that no prophecy of scripture is a matter of one's own interpretation* (2 Peter 1:20), so tradition puts us in touch with a long and ongoing conversation.

Experience, for Wesley, was the verification of biblical teaching in the lives of believers. We experience what the Bible promises. It was not simple feeling, as in "This works for me," as much as it was the fruit of the Spirit seen in one's life. But our experiences are *our* experiences. The authority of Scripture often means simply the authority of my interpretation. It's one thing to say the Bible is the highest source of Christian knowledge and quite another to know precisely what that knowledge is.

When the Bible seems to speak clearly to someone, as when a solution to a problem becomes apparent during devotional time, or when meditating on a passage, even though the answer is particularized in that moment, for that person and for that specific problem, there is an overwhelming urge to universalize it and claim it is THE answer for all time. These moments of insight are subjective and are often interpretations, themselves, of events, and should be carefully applied beyond ourselves.[18] Combined with tradition and reason, experience is a helpful tool.

17 A methodology for theological reflection suggested by John Wesley, leader of the Methodist movement, in the late 18th Century.

18 For a comprehensive treatment of the problems associated with personal communications from God, see Henry Neufeld, *When People Speak for God*, (Gonzolez Florida: Energion Publications), 2007.

N. T. Wright objects. "If 'experience' is in itself a *source* of authority, we can no longer be *addressed* by a word which comes from beyond ourselves. At this point, theology and Christian living cease to be rooted in God himself, and are rooted instead in our own selves; in other words, they become a form of idolatry in which we exchanged the truth about God for a human-made lie."[19] Wright seems to think that we can get information straight from God without human filtering or corruption. Since everything about humanity is filtered through our experience, I don't see how we can escape factoring experience into the equation.

Reason is never "pure" reason; it is always a product of how we perceive logic. Aristotle's "A is not B," is logical in some systems, but illogical in others, as Buddhists will tell you. However, we all must think, and we will do so from a particular point of view. What is reasonable to one may very well be repugnant to another. It is vital that we understand why we reason the way we do, and that no matter how well reasoned, our conclusions will not be pure. Reason is one way to keep the subjectivity of experience in check.

We have seen how ancient, medieval, and Reformation interpreters were influenced by the prevailing notions of what constituted truth in their day. Few today would give themselves wholeheartedly to Aristotle, Plato, or Ptolemy, but we are still drawn by a variety of influences to see the world in a certain way. It is inevitable that these influences will impact our interpretations of the Bible. Currently, the most followed theological systems of interpretation are the Evangelical, Liberal, Fundamentalist, Pentecostal/Charismatic, and Progressive. None of these arose out of a vacuum and none of these interprets out of a vacuum; they all suffer/benefit from their worldviews and are a product of them.

Evangelicalism is, historically speaking, the oldest of the modern theological approaches. We will then give an overview of Liberalism, Fundamentalism, Pentecostal/Charismatic, and Progressive approaches.

---

19   N.T Wright, *Scripture and the Authority of God*, (San Francisco: HarperCollins), 2013, p. 103.

Evangelicalism

The Protestant Reformation populated the landscape of Europe and America with various denominations and sects, many of which survive to our day. Lutherans, Presbyterians, Congregationalists, Methodists, Anglicans/Episcopal, Baptists, Quakers, Puritans, all emerged in Europe. And all of these transplanted themselves to America where they found a home and thrived. Although they were quite different in matters of church governance, worship structure, and theology, they were basically orthodox and at home with the great creeds. (Although some like the Baptists and Quakers would repudiate creeds as conditions of fellowship, they largely accepted what they taught.) In America beginning in the late 18th century, they cooperated in many evangelical revivals where "hitting the sawdust trail" was prominent. Calls for repentance and confession of Christ as savior rang out through the day and night. Which brings us to the name—Evangelical, or "bringers of the Good News of salvation." Evangelicals are largely defined by their uncompromising belief of salvation by faith in the atoning work of Jesus Christ and in the need to personally trust in Jesus to inherit eternal life.[20] Evangelicalism emerged out of the pietistic movement in Europe in the 18th century which still influences modern Evangelicals. Later, the great revivals of the 19th century fostered interdenominational cooperation that ushered in the early Missionary Societies. Foundational to the movement was its insistence on the need for conversion, the literal understanding of the Bible, the centrality of the death, burial and resurrection of Christ for salvation, an activist spirit that led to missionary activity at home and abroad, and social reform movements.[21] The more conservative largely ignored or castigated the emerging critical tools for biblical research. They took the Bible at face value and saw no

---

20 George Marsden, *Understanding Fundamentalism and Evangelicalism*, (Grand Rapids: Wm. B. Eerdmans Publishing Co.), 1991, p. 2.
21 It's not well known that the author of *In His Steps*, Charles Sheldon, was an Evangelical and promoter of the Social Gospel.

need to look deeper,[22] although there were others who welcomed aspects of critical inquiry seeing in them ways to uphold the Bible.

In the latter half of the 20th century, due to the infighting over dispensational premillennialism[23] and adoption of some of the higher critical methods, what Harold Okenga called the "New Evangelicals" emerged under the leadership of Billy Graham and Fuller Theological Seminary. What is significant here, for our purposes, is that this split among former allies was due to differences in the attitude they took to interpreting the Bible. Bray summarizes the difference: "Are there pre-programmed answers to every question, or is there freedom to discover new truths in the Scriptures?"[24] Conservative Evangelicals (soon to be known as Fundamentalists) looked to defend the Bible while Evangelicals looked to learn from it. So much of the interpretive outcome depends on what you bring to the Bible.

Liberalism

Liberalism cannot be understood apart from the Enlightenment and its presuppositions. It emerged just following the Reformation. The Enlightenment was also known as the Age of Reason, as it championed the notion that all problems could be solved by the rigorous application of logic.[25] It saw Tradition as unenlightened, even superstitious. Therefore it disregarded the assured teachings of the church and began the search for truth independent of dogmatic presumptions. Significant is its use of the emerging "scientific method" which emphasized objective truth obtained through (presumably) objective research. Enlightenment Liberals approached biblical interpretation the same way they approached any literature. Although they often differed in approaches, they

22 Marsden, *op. cit*, p. 75.
23 Popularized in Hal Lindsey's 1970s bestseller, *The Late, Great Planet Earth* and through the *Left Behind Series* by Tim Lahaye and Jerry Jenkins
24 Bray, *op. cit.*, p. 555.
25 John Dillenberger and Claude Welch, *Protestant Christianity*, 2nd ed., (New York: Macmillan Publishing Company, 1988), p. 162.

were united in their pursuit of tolerance, a strong belief in human progress, and resisting the abuses of the State and religion.

Not all early Enlightenment figures were atheists or deists. Some were committed Christians, but held views not considered orthodox. However, they looked askance at miracles, the incarnation, bodily resurrection, revelation and the like: anything that couldn't be proved with reason. Therefore, they worked to find the essence of Christianity, or that which in the final analysis could be the logical core of the faith free from dogmatic assertions and coerced belief.

This is where the method called biblical criticism (also known as historical criticism) emerges. Its purpose was to answer many of the questions which arose in the minds of many thinking readers of the Bible but were not taken seriously by the church. Examples include why Matthew, Mark, and Luke (the Synoptic Gospels) are so different from John. Why are the Synoptics seeming repetitions of each other? How could Moses have written the Pentateuch when he describes his own death and burial? How can miracles be explained?

Given that Enlightenment scholars were working from a worldview that did not include the possibility of miracles, they had to find alternatives to explain them. A leading example is Jesus' feeding of the 5,000 as recorded in all four Gospels. Jesus is said to have "multiplied" a few loaves and fishes donated by a boy from the crowd, into sufficient numbers to feed the entire crowd and have twelve basketsful left over. An impressive feat indeed. One suggested alternative explanation to a miracle is that the generosity of the boy, who was willing to share his lunch, prompted others in the crowd to share their hidden lunches to such an extent that all were fed. In these interpreters' eyes, this was just as impressive a "miracle" as the other.

Among liberals was the belief that God is love. That is to say, that love is not simply an attribute of God's nature, but that the essence of God's being is love. This love means that God is primarily immanent, close to the creation, rather than transcendent and remote. This produced a belief in universalism, that God would not condemn anyone to a literal hell. A God who is love would not, therefore, condemn all at birth (Original Sin), either.

But it is the idea of progress, that "every day, in every way, the world is getting better and better," that typifies liberal Christianity through the 19th century. There was great optimism that a truly Christian society could be created. Prosperity was at its highest, the Theory of Evolution was seen as progressive and continuous improvement, the world was largely at peace, nature was being subdued, medical advances were ending many diseases with the promise of ending many more, and humanity was on the way to perfectibility. Sin, it seemed, was no longer a useful description of the human predicament. All this was but a prelude to the coming of Fundamentalist Christianity.

Fundamentalism

Emerging out of 19th century Evangelicalism is a subset known as Fundamentalism. Coming on the heels of Liberalism, the more conservative members of Evangelicalism sought to defend the faith against liberal inroads. During the rise of biblical criticism a re-action set in, which shouldn't be much of a surprise. Many of the revered teachings/interpretations of the Bible were challenged, including the Virgin Birth of Jesus, the inerrancy of the Bible, mir-acles, substitutionary atonement, the literal resurrection of Christ, and the Second Coming of Christ. The ascendance of the Theory of Evolution challenged the literalness of a six day creation and of Adam and Eve. So between 1909 and 1915 a group of conservative scholars from mostly Baptist and Presbyterian seminaries produced a twelve volume work called *The Fundamentals*, and "Fundamen-talists" were born.

The foundational doctrine for Fundamentalists then and now is called the verbal, plenary inspiration of the Bible. It's the belief that God "breathed" the words into the biblical writers, and there-fore it is free from error in every way. So all statements regarding science ("In the beginning...."), history (the sun stopped its jour-ney over Jericho), geography (the Flood), biography (Methuselah was 969 years old) and the like, are taken at face value and considered not just true, but irreproachable. In fact, their defense of inerrancy is so strong that many believe that if one biblical fact is disproven, none of it can be taken seriously.[26]

Postmodernism's insistence (in the extreme) that the world, reality, and even the individual are ultimately unknowable, is how N. T. Wright explains the recent rise of fundamentalism. "This uncertainty of course, begets a new and anxious eagerness for certainty: hence, the appeal of fundamentalism, which in today's world is not so much a return to the premodern worldview, but precisely to one form of modernism (reading the Bible within a grid of a pseudoscientific quest for objective truth)."[27]

Most Fundamentalists think they are following in the tradition and beliefs of the early church. It should be apparent by now that the early church had no consensus of beliefs and that their methods of interpreting the Bible hardly coincide. What Fundamentalists are working from is an Enlightenment notion that truth is objective and it can be discovered through human reason. In applying this to the Bible, by way of John Locke and others, it is seen as a huge repository of truth that can be mined with the right tools. Hence, their Bible is treated as a giant source book for the discovery of propositions that are turned into doctrinal statements. Naturally this sets up conditions for doctrinal wars that continue to separate out the "true believers" from the false. For Fundamentalists often fall prey to the notion that, "Since I derived this meaning straight from the Bible, it is equal in force to the Bible itself." Now try to argue with that![28] This approach has divided and anathematized fellow Fundamentalists from the start. One such wing, the Premi-

---

26 The doctrine of an inerrant Bible seems to suggest that interpretations may as well be inerrant. But who is to make that judgment? The Bible may well be inerrant, but there are no inerrant interpreters.

27 N.T Wright, *op. cit.*, p. 7.

28 R. W. Dale noted as early as 1889 "that to put a meaning of [one's] own into a Bible sentence and to claim Divine authority for it, was just as bad as to put a sentence of [one's] own into the Bible and to claim Divine authority for it." *The Old Evangelicalism and the New* (London, 1889), pp. 23–25.

llennialists (the belief in a 1000 year reign of Jesus on Earth), have three different views of the timing of what they call the Rapture (when Jesus returns for his church prior to the millennium). They also propose a seven year Tribulation that is connected, somehow, to the timing of the Rapture. Will the Rapture be pre-Tribulation (the 3½ years preceding the Rapture)? mid-Tribulation (during the Tribulation)? Or post-Tribulation (self-explanatory)? It's not so much that they maintain these conflicting views as it is that, in extreme cases, those with other views are condemned to hell for not believing the Bible, when in fact the others are just as sure *they* are the ones who believe the Bible. Of course, condemning other Christians is as old as Christianity and as recent as today.[29]

Pentecostal/Charismatic

Although efforts to "restore the church of the New Testament" began in Europe with the Anabaptists and English Puritans, they took off in earnest in America as part of the Holiness revivals of the 19th century. Pentecostals find the evidence for a restored church in the supernatural signs of God's presence as seen in a congregation's exercise of spiritual gifts, especially faith healings and speaking in tongues. Beginning in 1906 and continuing through 1915, a revival at the Azusa Street Mission in Los Angeles was described as witnessing healings, tongues, miracles, and enthusiastic worship, what many would call a replication of the Day of Pentecost in Acts 2. Hence the name Pentecostal. Many attendees returned to their own churches with the message of the Azusa revival, and Pentecostal churches began springing up across the nation. Soon the Assemblies of God formed a denomination, to be followed by the Church of God (Cleveland, Tennessee), the Church of God in Christ, and the Pentecostal Holiness Church, as well as many independent congregations.

Evangelical church leaders were quick to criticize this new movement. Most believed that the age of miracles had ceased with

---

29   Consider John MacArthur's scathing condemnation of Rob Bell as a false teacher in a recent blog. http://www.gty.org/Blog/B110412.

23

the deaths of the apostles, so these "outpourings" are either of the devil[30], or psychologically induced. They also worried that the authority of the Bible would be undermined if people believed that they got direct communication from God. The passage of time has shown that their fears were largely unwarranted, except in extreme cases, and much cooperation between Evangelicals and Pentecostals is in evidence throughout the world. Beginning in the 1960s and 1970s, most of the Mainline Protestant Churches and many Roman Catholic congregations had members who claimed possession of spiritual gifts (charismata), and are known as charismatic Christians.

Given their roots in the Holiness movement, with its strong emphasis on the experience of sanctification, Pentecostals lean more on the experience leg of the Wesleyan Quadrilateral. But because they are essentially biblical literalists, they tend to agree with the doctrines of the Evangelicals.

The modern movement to restore the New Testament Church has taken many turns.[31] Pentecostals emphasize gifts of the Spirit, Churches of Christ emphasize church governance practices, and Holiness groups emphasize restoring the high standards of ethical behavior of the New Testament. In interpreting the Bible, each approach is based on a perceived emphasis that is prior to and dominates the field. We are entitled to ask what it is about individuals or communities that lead them to emphasize one over another. The partial answer is that more than a simple appeal to the Bible is at work here.

---

30 C. Campbell Morgan called Pentecostals, "the last vomit of Satan," as noted by Harvey Cox in his *The Future of Faith*, (New York: HarperOne, 2009), p. 201.

31 It is ironic in the extreme that the leading Restoration Movement group of congregations known as the Churches of Christ normally disfellowship anyone who claims gifts of the Spirit. Since they believe the Apostolic era, with its miracles, etc., is not recoverable, they end up restoring the church of the 2nd century (if that)!

Progressive

Progressive Christian thought is often described as the theology of Postmodernism. It is tied to the worldview where everything is connected and all things influence each other. The universe is a closed system where God is entirely immanent and in many cases only metaphorically transcendent (wholly other). This makes it very compatible with panentheism (the belief that God exists "in with and under" everything, but is at the same time, transcendent of everything). It is distinct from pantheism which sees God as the sum total of everything.

There is in the intellectual world a phenomenon akin to Newton's Third Law of Motion. "For every action there is an equal and opposite reaction." Progressive Christian thought emerged partly in reaction to the Christian (Fundamentalist) Right's rise to political power in America. In the process, they claimed to be the only true representative of Christianity, a notion Progressives resented. They also see their work as a corrective to the excesses of Liberal Christianity.

Since Progressive Christianity is a relatively new movement, there is no such thing as an official description, only tendencies. However, there are several lines of thought that can be said to form a pattern of thinking shared by many.

Liberalism, they argue, lost contact with the heart of the Christian story in an effort to accommodate Modernism. It defined Christianity in such a way that it became undifferentiated from a social movement, and transitioned from a religion into a philosophy of religion. The Progressive corrective is to reclaim the heart of the biblical story as our story (admittedly reinterpreted), ground our theology in the incarnation of God in Jesus, and return the church to be servants of the world. It also sees the Bible and tradition as authoritative voices that must be listened to critically, while understanding that both are human products, full of wisdom as well as fraught with danger.

The foundational belief that the incarnation holds the interpretive clue to understanding ourselves, our world, and God, leads many Progressives to Process Theology.

25

Most of us are members of a particular denomination because we were born into it. At least that's the way it's been until recently when Baby Boomers began reemerging in the churches after a long absence (nicknamed the Baby Boomerang). Many went back to the churches of their youth, but many did not. And since the decline of the mainline denominations, which began in the 1970s, nondenominational or independent "Bible-believing" churches have arisen that have attracted millions. For those who returned, or never left, their denominations provide a safe haven where they are nurtured on denomination-specific beliefs and attitudes that are rarely challenged. When challenged, it is rarely done on the basis of solid biblical objections but on vague charges of being "too liberal," or "too conservative," politically. But whether born into or converted into a faith tradition, the typical lay member is not concerned with the substantial history of the development of its dogma; so whatever beliefs are crucial to that tradition are taken for granted as sufficiently true.

There is also a large body of "whatever church is convenient, mostly for my kids." For them, denominational nuances are irrelevant. A study from Gray Matter found that Protestant churchgoers are no more loyal to their church denomination than they are to their brand of toothpaste.[32] Many observers see this as good (old rivalries are diminishing) and bad (old rivalries are diminishing). This underscores that for most people, arguing over the Bible is either unnecessary at the least and counterproductive at the worst.

Many people who are disaffected by their former denomination find their way into so-called nondenominational churches that bill themselves as "Bible believing." The implication, of course, is that they have interpreted the Bible correctly and others haven't, or don't care about the Bible at all. Ironically, "Bible believing churches" can't seem to agree on just what it is that the Bible teaches. They regularly debate one another, condemn one another, and steal each

---

32 http://www.greymatterresearch.com/index_files/Denominational_ Loyalty.htm

other's members. This is one more indication that the Bible isn't that easy to understand, and that people easily think it is.

CHAPTER 3
LIVING WITH OUR DISAGREEMENTS:
HOW SHOULD WE PROCEED?

HOW DO OUR ATTITUDES AFFECT
HOW WE INTERPRET THE BIBLE?

By now it should be readily apparent that outside influences have a bearing on what we take from the Bible. I'm reminded of the story of the desert traveler who happened upon an old man at a city gate. "What kind of people will I find in your city," he enquired? "What kind did you find where you came from," was his reply? "Knaves, fools, thieves and beggars," shot back the traveler. To which the old man replied, "These you will find in our city."

Moments later another traveler arrived at the city gate with the same question for the old man. "What kind did you find where you came from," was his reply? "Good hearted, generous, welcoming and helpful," said the traveler. "These you will find in our city," answered the old man.

One of the many human predispositions that interfere with our approach to the Bible is known in psychology as "confirmation bias," the tendency to search for information that conforms to our wishes and desired outcomes and overlooks or downplays any evidence to the contrary.[33] It's been characterized as "We believe what we want to believe," and therefore we find what we want to find. This is especially true when we work from a theological point of view that we are committed to upholding (as opposed to holding an hypothesis and evaluating the evidence). Having committed beliefs is not only appropriate, but virtually impossible to avoid. The issue is to recognize that we have this tendency and seek to control it as best as we can. One way to recognize its presence is that we confirm a prior understanding upon a first reading. This may be nothing more than our bias at work; it needs to be examined more carefully.

---

33 Jonathan Baron, *Thinking and Deciding*, (New York: Cambridge University Press), 3rd ed., pp. 162-164.

Disagreement is inevitable and therefore necessary. Necessary? Yes, as it points to the limitations of the human capacity to discern ultimate truth. It's another way of acknowledging that we need each other. Your strengths may shore up my weaknesses and vice versa. But this can only happen if we allow it to. Disagreements often arise because some interpreters fail to recognize their own baggage that they bring to the task, and believe they are operating in a "baggage free zone," where one's assumptions, if they are thought of at all, are assumed to be true, untainted by human error.

Even biblical scholars are subject to interpreting from their own biases. "Anyone who has worked within biblical scholarship knows, or ought to know, that we biblical scholars come to the text with just as many interpretive strategies and expectations as anyone else, and that integrity consists not of having no presuppositions but in being aware of what one's presuppositions are and of the obligation to listen to and interact with those who have different ones."[34] Where one's interpretive assumptions are recognized as well as those with whom they disagree, more room for accommodation and reconsideration is present. So our disagreements are less about what the Bible means than with the various milieus from which they spring. Since there is no such thing as a certifiably perfect milieu, we should welcome another's interpretation as a necessary contribution to the whole. The foregoing chapters are intended to make this clear. Given this reality, we are better able to address one another as an equal rather than as an "other."

HUMILITY AS OUR GUIDE:
DO WE REALLY LISTEN TO EACH OTHER?

Confirmation bias is but one of the many ways humans deceive themselves and is operative across the interpretive spectrum. Another very human trait is to push harder in the face of contrary evidence. A recent study by two psychologists scientifically confirmed this reality by conducting three experiments where

---

34   N.T Wright, *op. cit.*, (San Francisco: HarperCollins, 2013), p. 13.

evidence was introduced that negated strongly held convictions. The reaction? Not acquiescence in the face of solid evidence, but doubling down on their insistence that they were right. The title of the study? "When in Doubt, Shout!: Paradoxical Influences of Doubt on Proselytizing."[35]

Disagreeing can be either a learning experience for one or both, or another way of missing the point of loving one's neighbor as one's self. As Henry Neufeld put it, "You are never more God-like than when you open your heart's door to another person. The more different they are, the more God-like that action is."[36] Neufeld's understanding of God makes possible such an outcome. Another view of God, much less grace-full, might wish for a more violent outcome, as for those who want gays and lesbians executed in the name of their God. Once again, what we take to the Bible informs what we take out of the Bible.

Truly listening to each other is a difficult task because it makes us vulnerable. Listening at its heart is opening up oneself to the possibility of change. If we are not vulnerable, we are not really listening. Humility is the willingness to learn, the acknowledgement that not all is known, and the mark of a true disciple.

What does it say about our faith if our beliefs keep us from working together? In other words, do we place such importance on "my way" that we keep good works from happening? Or, are we more committed to our beliefs than to our mission? The judgment scene in Matthew 25 is most instructive. The criterion for being called to Jesus' side is not what we believe but what we do in his name. Paul tells us that knowledge of God's will is for the purpose of creating good works (Col. 1:9-10), rather than puff us up (1 Cor. 13). Then there's James' warning that even the demons believe, but tremble.

Diversity of opinion may well be a fact of creation, for God seems to love diversity. Andrew Village suggests that the Parable of

35   David Gal and Derek D. Rucker, *Psychological Science* 2010 21: 1701-1708.
36   Henry Neufeld, *Not Ashamed of the Gospel: Confessions of a Liberal Charismatic,* (Gonzalez, Florida: Energion Publications) 2005, p. 32.

the Talents, with its allocation of differing "talents"[37] among people, is a model for understanding differing interpretations.[38] Every effort at putting our talents to work is rewarded by the master. One should not disparage the efforts of a two talent person who doesn't achieve the interpretive brilliance of the ten talent person, but find value in the effort, if not in the outcome. That way, the integrity of the interpreter is upheld in spite of what differences may remain.

Not getting the Bible right in some of its particulars is hardly on the level of not getting our lives right. It seems that some in Matthew 25 got their lives right without knowing the particulars of why.

A MODEST PROPOSAL

Wright characterizes the interpretive task thusly: "We must be committed to a *totally contextual* reading of Scripture. Each word must be understood within its own verse, each verse within its own chapter, each chapter within its own book, and each book within its own historical cultural and indeed canonical setting."[39] One of the issues of biblical interpretation that describes this challenge of coming to a complete understanding of any text is called the hermeneutical circle. It posits that in order to understand a single verse, one must first understand the entire Bible, but to understand the entire Bible, one must first understand each verse. This, of course, is an impossibility. Therefore, many have suggested a way of drawing from the Bible the useful and identifying the not so useful, irrelevant, and downright harmful. It's called a canon within the Canon. This is an effort to approximate or summarize the essence of biblical teaching for the purpose of comparing portions of the Bible to it. Those who argue for this are not trying to eliminate any of the books of the Bible, *a la* Luther and Marcion, or remove any

---

37   Village notes that the Oxford English Dictionary finds that "talents" as natural human abilities, springs directly from this parable. Andrew Village, *The Bible and Lay People*, (Hanpshire, England: Ashgate Publishing Ltd., 2007), p. 167.
38   Andrew Village, *Ibid*, p. 166.
39   N. T. Wright, *op. cit.*, p. 128.

of its offending parts, such as Thomas Jefferson. In fact, it's just the opposite. It's intended to help the reader evaluate all its parts in a hierarchy of values.

A canon (not to be confused with cannon) is a means of measuring. The word "canon" comes from the Greek word meaning "rule" or "measuring stick". The sixty-six books that make up the Bible is the Canon of (Protestant) Christianity because it is used to measure all things in the faith. Edward W. H. Vick summarizes how this works:

"(1) The church makes selections from the Scriptures, giving greater importance to some passages than to others. (2) It often employs Scripture to support and to endorse the doctrines it teaches. (3) Certain of these doctrines come to have an importance above others. Hence the Scripture which 'supports' such central doctrine assumes special significance."[40]

Jonathan Pennington makes the case that we all have a canon within the Canon and proposes using the Gospels for that purpose. "My point with the 'canon within the Canon' language is that we in fact all do have certain verses, biblical books, and concepts that are operative, formative, and weightiest in our theological constructions. I simply want to suggest that, based on the early church's practice and for several other theological and canonical reasons, the fourfold Gospel book should serve in this lodestar role.[41]

For Luther, his canonical rule was Jesus Christ.[42] Whatever in the Bible did not measure up to his understanding of Jesus was considered unworthy for Christian consumption. That's how he was able to argue for the removal of the books of Hebrews, James, Jude and Revelation from the Bible; they didn't sufficiently display Christ.

Some think Jesus created a canon within the Canon when he summed up the entire Old Testament in answering the question of which commandment is the greatest. "Teacher, which command-

---

40　*From Inspiration to Understanding*, (Gonzales, Florida: Energion Publications, 2011), p. 9.
41　http://thegospelcoalition.org/blogs/trevinwax/2012/10/25/the-gospel-in-the-gospels-a-conversation-with-jonathan-pennington/
42　John Dillenberger and Claude Welsh, *op. cit.*, p. 40.

ment in the law is the greatest?" He said to him, "'You shall love the Lord your God with all your heart, and with all your soul, and with all your mind.' This is the greatest and first commandment. And a second is like it: 'You shall love your neighbor as yourself.' **On these two commandments hang all the law and the prophets**" (Matthew 22:36-40 emphasis mine).

I think Jesus was teaching us that if we keep these two great commandments in mind when studying the Old Testament (and even the New Testament), we can determine how best to live. For instance, slavery was condoned under the Law, just to name one example. However, if we keep the injunction to "love your neighbor as yourself" within that system, it would make slavery humane if not finally irrelevant.

In the final analysis, the validity of biblical interpretation may turn on this simple notion. Theologians have sought for generations to discover the unifying principle of the Bible and fail to achieve consensus. There is not even a consensus on the unifying principle of either the Old or New Testaments. Why? Because the various components that make up these Testaments don't speak with one voice. Proposed solutions always ignore parts that simply don't fit. This is true, as well, of the canon within the Canon. The best that we can do is choose wisely among the options and live with humility in the presence of others. Another way putting this is that we listen to what to us sounds like the voice of God and subordinate all other voices to it. We may as well, because that's what we do anyway. Now it's official!

CONSIDERATIONS WHEN APPROACHING THE BIBLE

Adopt a prayerful attitude of listening to scripture: you are the disciple, it is the teacher. Yes, the Holy Spirit is our teacher, but we can easily slip into the error of believing that anything we think we understand is a direct imparting from the Spirit. We must learn to distinguish our inner bias voice from that.

Be open to discovery: Don't tell the Bible what's there; discover it for yourself. Too often we begin with an agenda of proving something right when we should be open to discovering whatever is there for us. There are numerous books that will educate us in the many ways of doing this. Remember that even these have biases. All you can do is do your best, so do your best.

Leave assumptions aside: You've heard verses interpreted the same way for so long that you no longer listen to them. Give different viewpoints a hearing. One especially good way to do this is to find a conversation partner you don't agree with who is willing to discuss things with you with an open mind. Truly listening to one another will open many doors of understanding.

Reserve your judgment: Hold your conclusions tentatively and mull them over for a period of time before camping on them. Run them by several trusted people and see what results.

Be collaborative: Working in a vacuum of one is to cut oneself off from the vast repository of interpretive possibilities that are beyond any one person's reach. It's also a tacit admission of hubris.

Be open to revision of previously held notions: New information requires new thinking.

Follow the Golden Rule. Don't allow differences of outcomes to come between you and another created in the image of God. Always bear in mind that you are not the one another is called to please.

IT IS IMPERATIVE WE FIND A WAY TO LIVE TOGETHER IN SPITE OF DISAGREEING

The Protestant heritage of the priesthood of all believers with each person's right to their own biblical interpretation led to this cacophony of voices which has divided Christendom down to our day. What might we expect in the future? Certainly, if nothing changes, the divisiveness of the churches and the diminution of their influence in the world will continue. The response from a friend as I attempted to wean him from his atheism is typical of many in our day: "When you guys can get together on what the Bible says, maybe I'll listen. Not until then."

The reality of differences must not be seen as fundamentally bad. Surely, if the Bible can argue with itself, interpreters of the Bible are allowed that privilege as well. There would certainly be

34

something fundamentally wrong if all humans thought alike. Since we are all unique, we bear the marks of our uniqueness in our different approaches to life. Truly, variety is the spice of life.

Where we go wrong, it seems to me, is not respecting human finitude. If we begin with the proposition that regardless of the beauty and sublimity of a particular interpretation, there is no perfect, absolute, final understanding. Even though we may reach profound heights, we still see in a mirror, dimly. The threat to the church is not different outcomes, but those who would insist on their particular understanding at the expense of all others. The "one who knows" is like the person holding one piece of the jigsaw puzzle believing it's the whole picture. Paul warned us about those who think of themselves more highly than they ought. Humility before the Bible is a prime requisite of meaningful interpretation. Diversity (spice) is inevitable, and to try to force everyone into the same mold is not only futile, it goes against what it means to be human.

IN CONCLUSION

A Jewish theologian settled this question for me years ago. In his *I and Thou*, Martin Buber taught us the difference between treating a person as a human being (a Thou—one like yourself) or an object (an It—a thing to be used)[43]. If our purpose in biblical discussion is to win someone over, we no longer treat our conversationalist as a person, but as a thing to dominate. If, on the other hand, our objective is to discover something valuable and give our conversation partner an opportunity to teach us, we and our partner are one, or I/ Thou.

Perhaps the interpretive quest comes down to a simple question: Would you rather be right or righteous? Needing to be right pits you against all others when the inevitable differences arise. In the extreme, this makes *your opinion* more important than *the person* with whom you disagree. Is this any way to honor the image of God that we all share? Rather than insist on your point of view,

43   Martin Buber, *I and Thou*, first published in German in 1923 and in English in 1937.

inquire as to why a person holds a different view and how it helps that person live in the sight of God. After all, we learn not to appear scholarly, or erudite, or to win arguments, but to follow Jesus as a faithful disciple. That's the difference between being right and righteous. It's also the point of why we study the Bible in the first place. *Soli Deo Gloria.*

TOPICAL LINE DRIVES

Straight to the Point in under 44 Pages

All Topical Line Drives volumes are priced at $4.99 print and 99¢ in all ebook formats.

Available

Forthcoming

Planned

(The titles of planned volumes may change before release.)

Generous Quantity Discounts Available
Dealer Inquiries Welcome
Energion Publications — P.O. Box 841
Gonzalez, FL 32560
Website: http://energionpubs.com
Phone: (850) 525-3916

www.ingramcontent.com/pod-product-compliance
Lightning Source LLC
Chambersburg PA
CBHW011748020426
42331CB00014B/3327